# HOMECOMING

## POEMS

## DENMIT LEPCHA NAMCHU

Copyright © Denmit Lepcha Namchu
All Rights Reserved.

This book has been self-published with all reasonable efforts taken to make the material error-free by the author. No part of this book shall be used, reproduced in any manner whatsoever without written permission from the author, except in the case of brief quotations embodied in critical articles and reviews.

The Author of this book is solely responsible and liable for its content including but not limited to the views, representations, descriptions, statements, information, opinions and references ["Content"]. The Content of this book shall not constitute or be construed or deemed to reflect the opinion or expression of the Publisher or Editor. Neither the Publisher nor Editor endorse or approve the Content of this book or guarantee the reliability, accuracy or completeness of the Content published herein and do not make any representations or warranties of any kind, express or implied, including but not limited to the implied warranties of merchantability, fitness for a particular purpose. The Publisher and Editor shall not be liable whatsoever for any errors, omissions, whether such errors or omissions result from negligence, accident, or any other cause or claims for loss or damages of any kind, including without limitation, indirect or consequential loss or damage arising out of use, inability to use, or about the reliability, accuracy or sufficiency of the information contained in this book.


Made with ♥ on the Notion Press Platform
www.notionpress.com

# Preface

In 2021, amid the COVID-19 pandemic, I wrote my first book, Lee. A book that dives into many aspects of human life but especially that of healing and one's journey towards self-love. Lee was my journey of going through the bad and ugly and eventually forgiving myself and returning to the place where I always belonged, to the home in my heart.

(An excerpt from Lee)

**You've wandered enough,**

**You've slept in many arms,**

**Lived in many hearts,**

**And the journey back home is a difficult one.**

**But make it anyway,**

**Stay, stay,**

**Because you've forgotten that home**

**Is in your own arms.**

After I had vented my aches and healed, fast forward, I was in a better place, living a good life thinking I never had to battle with those feelings of loneliness and dejection ever again. But I was wrong and it all came back unanticipatedly sooner than I had expected it to, leading me to exactly where I was 3 years ago. The voices in my head would not settle until I penned it all down, and that is how Homecoming was born.

Homecoming is a book of poems divided into 3 chapters: The Running, The Returning and The Healing. Through these poems on love, grief, self-love and discovery, I want my readers to know that healing and hurting are the two sides of the same coin and returning home is a journey one has to embark on time and again in their life, but what remains constant is that Home will never abandon you.

Happy Homecoming.

# Acknowledgements

Thanks to Samden for designing the stunning book cover, and bringing my vision to life.

Thanks to the team at Notion Press for the seamless publishing process.

Thank you book store owners Raman from Rachna Books, Lekha from Café The Twins and Manisha from The Travel Café for selling my books without the slightest hesitation.

Thanks to Anom Chezang and Lungming, for reviewing my manuscript and providing valuable feedback.

Thank you peace for finding me amid war.

Thank you home for always letting me in during the storm.

And I can't thank you enough, my dear readers for your immeasurable love and support.

*To all those on their way back home.*

*This book is about the Running, the Returning and the Healing.*

*Because superheroes aren't real*
*Only poets will save the world.*

*I wrote you a song*
*But since I can't sing*
*I called it a poem.*

THE RUNNING

# 1

Sleep love,
Shut your moons,
And since it's a sin to
Love you by daylight,
I'll love you by the night.
You'll see me in your dreams
But don't you open your eyes
From the scent of me
You'll know that I've come
To sin, yet another time
And if you can,
Without uttering a word
Secretly, silently
Forgive me,
Secretly, silently the way I'll always love you.

# 2

In the lap of Autumn
On the brink of winter
I shed my skin
Like the leaves
To wear a thicker one
To survive the snow
And your coldness.

# 3

The man on the moon is drunk tonight
It can't stand on its two feet
But the clouds keep
Covering for its sins
Only showing light,
Playing hide and seek.
Maybe it's not for the drunk moon
But for all those children
Who still believe in fairy tales
And the brighter side of things,
Not knowing the moon shines
Out of borrowed light,
On the cold side of daylight.

# 4

Even in the wake of memory,
You were,
Just an illusion.

# 5

The tree is naked,
Autumn has come and gone.
But your memories linger on
Like the one-leaf
Refusing to fall
But it's only it's fate
To be on the ground.
Surrendering through an act of humble submission
Marking the start of winter,
And the coldest nights
Where Spring is a distant mirage.
And the summer sun shining only on a faraway land
Makes me want to go into hibernation
My period of dormancy
For the next three months,
Or months after.
Because the Winter wind weakens my bones
And to Hope
Is a task too tiring for the heart.

# 6

Today I sit down to write something
But no thoughts come to me
I want to sing a song
But no tune
Reverberates on my tongue,
I want to dance a dance,
But there's no movement in my bones.
I sit still on my window sill
And watch the cherry tree
Swaying its branches
In the gentlest ways,
It dances before my eyes,
The birds warble
Hymns of nature,
Soothing my sorrows.
I realise that it is my duty
And I must write
So I write about the cherry tree
Opening up its buds
On the brink of winter
Even after it's shed all its leaves.
We are all created by the cosmos,
And we must abide by its laws

And trust,

That we can survive any winter,

Just as the trees do,

Just like the birds.

# 7

How can I ever be full
On my own,
When I'm merely half a moon
Without you
Waiting for the other half to join in
Before I can be full again.
Another twenty-eight days,
Went by like a year
Or years,
The cycle should repeat
But it never did
And there shone all kinds of moons on my sky
Half and crescent,
Gibbous and new.
But the two halves never met
And the full moon never shone
Above my bed
Maybe they were better off
As one shining during the day,
And the other by the night.
Like shining on two different skies.

# 8

How do you know what freedom is
When you've always been caged ?

# 9

When home abandons you,

An inch,

A meter,

A mile all look the same.

# 10

The fault was ours
Forever was just too easy to blame.

# 11

Keep your heart cold
You are not a fire
To light everyone's house
Or to warm everyone's body
You are not a refuge
For everyone to come in
During the storm
And leave
As soon as the day
Begins to show
And the sun begins to shine.

# 12

I want to meet you in every place I ever go
To be filled by your presence
And all the years we had
Went by like seconds
And all the long years
Were the times
I wept in your absence.

# 13

Why has the rain ceased
And the flowers returned
Why does the chirping bird
Sound so happy
At the sight of the fooling sun?
I crave for the October winds,
And the crispy September leaves.
I crave for carefree days,
And nights catching stars.
Oh, ugly Summer!
Wake me up when you're gone.
No, I don't want to look pretty
With white daisies in my head
And dresses that just hit the thighs.
Promise me a slower August,
And the longest November nights.

# 14

We burned like fire,
But now tears are all we have.
The flames long put out.
The story ended.
Only the tingling sensation,
Of memories remain,
Kindling a spark,
Out of the ashes,
The burnt remains,
Of your letter,
Half ablaze,
Your picture,
Half torn,
Taped back,
Your smile crooked,
It now looks like a frown.
Mourning over a love lost,
A lover dead.
A Grief found,
To remain.
In your place.

# 15

Who are you that comes so late at night
And vanishes at the subtlest sight of dawn
In this heaviness of sleep
You are but a mere dream.

# 16

Our hearts are empty
All the love has been taken

*(For granted)*

# 17

I am but a flickering light
That comes and goes
You need someone who loves you consistently
What is the use of always being there
Like the moon.
When on some days
I can't even make myself visible to you.

# 18

Amber and pear,

Golden sun, raisin sweet,

There's a fire in your bones

That turns mine into metal.

Ash blonde highlights

I thought you said

Was the colour you turned

Your hair into.

And Iris, the colour of your eyes.

I wildly run through the trees,

And dance in the rain

But bathe in the moonlight,

Looking for a cup of lemon tea

And a street littered with Laburnum trees,

But I return to you, Oh! Fire,

To colour my white roses yellow

I think I was born on the wrong planet,

I always wanted to be born on Mars.

# 19

Love is too sweet,
It's sweetness can only be measured
By the pain it causes afterwards.

# 20

I introduced you to poetry,
As if I always knew,
There would be days when,
We would no longer be together.
And a poem would be the only way
To stay close to you
Only a few words apart.

# 21

How do you expect
A writer to look like
Old and shabby
Reeking of books?
Talking to a dying leaf
Amid fall,
Revisiting shattered homes,
And shattered dreams,
Eyes on the verge of closing
Looking for another muse.
She is putting a dress on her grief
Sometimes a black one,
Sometimes white
And sometimes just stark naked.
Writers are vain people,
Old and shabby,
Sweet and wild,
Until you're their next muse,
And you realise,
Writers are dangerous people.

# 22

My mother says,

It's winter!

It takes the longest time for a wound to heal in winter,

And the numb and cold finger hurt equally bad

But I love winters,

For I'm used to going back to what hurts,

And what takes forever to heal.

Your scent has not left my skin,

It clings to me like,

I'm under the ripest guava tree,

And I can't move anywhere,

It's cold,

And I don't want the warm air between us to evade

My fingers grow numb,

I can't pen letters to you,

That I'll stack under my bed,

It's cold and I ripe the guavas beneath two more blankets,

And watch from windows,

The marigolds littering the streets in yellow.

The marigolds bloom like they're mocking me

They bloom like they are exhilarated at your departure,

Swaying their heads, singing a farewell song.

The oranges here are the orangest,

You say, "It's absurd for an orange to be green."
The oranges here are the sweetest,
You don't like them sour.
We lay with our heads back,
Popping the oranges in our mouths,
Basking in the dying rays of the sun,
I'm in a dream,
Perhaps I had fallen asleep.
It's one of the heaviest
Like I'm intoxicated
With the smell of ripe guavas and marigolds and you,
I pick an orange and pop it in my mouth,
It's sour,
I open my eyes,
You're not next to me,
The sun has set,
I'm cold and isolated.
You've run away with the sweetest, ripest oranges,
Leaving the rotting guavas and marigolds behind.
My eyes are hazy,
Full of tears.
Our bond, I thought was still full of years.
My mom yells, "Be careful!"
But by then the red drips,
I have diced my heart again.
Into two.

# 23

My love is not a test
Of how bad of a heartbreak,
You could survive.
Nor is my love a lesson
For you to never love again,
Don't blame me,
I am but a vagabond,
Who cannot stay in one place,
I come and go,
Sometimes like thorns that prick your heart,
Other times like the waves,
That washes the blood away.

# 24

You're so loud and clear,
You want me.
But have you ever
Approached me with silence?
Have you for once loved;
Without wanting anything back?

# 25

We don't know how to love
In portions and proportions,
Once we start loving,
We give till our bones break,
And our hearts bleed.

# 26

Your memories would chase me
Everywhere I'd go
Until I realised,
It was but me
Who carried it
Everywhere I went.

# 27

To hold a heart,
And not break it,
To love someone
And not end up hurting them,
To miss someone so dearly
And not have them
For the rest of your life.

# 28

They say,
I have a stone heart
And yet it is so easy to cut
Even with words.

# 29

An almost person,
His half love,
Doesn't have to make
You feel like
You couldn't
Give enough.

# 30

Who is the one
Who taught me how to love,
Is it you mother?
Who makes me love,
Till my heart aches.

# 31

Maybe our maps were always different
Maybe where we met
Was just a border town
And we thought
Our paths would cross again.

# 32

Like the moon
The most beautiful things in life
Are far from your reach.
How can you persuade the moon to love you.
All you can do is admire it,
And watch it till it fades,
And wait for it to show up another night.
That too only if the clouds are kind enough
And not so Grey.

# 33

Sometimes, your memories hurt me
They hurt me more than just sometimes.
But I also know there will be days
When your words will no longer trigger me to write,
When your memories will no longer make me cry.
And then I will possibly miss being hurt
When I can no longer miss you
So then I think I am lucky to have loved you,
And to have been loved by you,
And to hurt and be hurt by you.
For pain is only an inevitable consequence of love
And I would rather hurt in love
Than not be loved at all
I would have rather known your good and evil
Than to have not known you at all.

# 34

After they licked the summer on your lips
Like an ice cream,
Who would not mind,
Falling into winter
Like it was spring.

# 35

I blamed you
For all these years
I have grieved
But now
realise
That all the wounds,
The cuts and bruises
Have come from me stabbing my own
heart
I have doubted myself
And soaked myself in tears of guilt.
Had I known
That the sword was in my own hands
I would have been more gentler
With myself
I would have used it as a rake instead
To grow a garden of love
But it's never too late,
I am sowing seeds this time.

# 36

How well do you know me,
Because the most naked you've seen me,
Is with this skin on.
Something beyond lies.
Forbidden, forgotten.
You've forgotten to look into the eyes.

# 37

It's a giant leap
Of a step I've taken
Now I'm not a part
Of both the worlds.

# 38

You can break,
But don't stay broken for too long,
Grief will take you as it's home.

# 39

What's there to fear
What's there to lose
Who I loved the most
Has already left.

# 40

All we have is this broken heart,
To stitch,
To mend
To break again.

# 41

What does the sun see in a sunflower?

What does a sculpture see in a stone?

Perhaps it's what I see in your eyes

Without my glasses on.

I did some laundry today,

Washing along the tinge of your fragrance,

That hung on the clothes I wore that night.

The sun is so warm,

Telling us exactly,

Why the week-long rain was necessary

The wine glass empties

One after another,

It feels like the start

But it's already over.

And all that's left with me

Are some memories,

A scar on my wrist

And a song marked as favourite

On my playlist.

# 42

I would burn myself to
Give you warmth,
But I know,
You would still come for my ashes.

# 43

You don't have to be the sun
For some body's sun flowers
When all they do
Is look away
As soon as it gets
Cold and dark.

# 44

Stay,
You're safe in between these pages,
My poetry is the closest thing to home,
I can make of.

# 45

Thats the thing about hearts
As long as it beats
It will bleed.

# 46

It's been a week
The sun is cold
Perhaps it forgot how to shine
After you left town.
How is it that the word
That struck you
Was spelt as g-r-i-e-f and not l-o-v-e.
The days were supposed to be golden,
The garden is full of white lilies,
The sky is a pale blue,
Threatening to pour,
Greys upon us.
The grey reminds me of the moon
Interlaced with the smoky clouds,
For a moment I forget,
Who I am,
I'm a bee, I'm a star
And I dance my heart away with the man on the moon.
I cannot think,
But I think that's what you become,
When you're intoxicated with grief,
It feels the same,
As being madly in love with you.

# 47

This heart is shattered into
A million little pieces
Hence, all that comes out,
Hurts and cuts.

# 48

Some people will
Always be eager
To fill other's cups
Even if theirs are empty
For this act of giving
Is a trait
That was born
As she was born.
And no one ever told her
She needed a refill
Before she could pour again.
And she will keep on pouring
Till it's depleted even of air
And it cracks and it breaks
But nothing drips.

# 49

Your love came in pieces
I didn't know
I could be whole.

# 50

But how could we last
It was in a world of oxymorons
We found each other
Where lies are sweet
And truths are bitter
How can a four-lettered word
Last a forever?

# 51

You owe me so much love,
Forevers and infinities will just be numbers.

# 52

If for a moment
I could hide between the pages of a book.

# 53

To write down
Is an act of remembrance
Perhaps
That's why my poetry
Has been attempting,
To cling on to the
Memory of you
Faded and hazy
I wrote and wrote
But could neither
Hold you
Nor the memory of you.

# 54

If there's one person
In this world that needs to be fixed
Then that is me,
I am holding the broken pieces in my heart,
And offering it to you,
Please come back,
And put me back together,
Make me whole,
For you know where the pieces will go,
For you are the one,
Who's broken that soul.

# 55

This rage has set,
Everything on fire
All we shared is burning,
The war has already begun.
I won't be able to save anything,
If I don't write it down.

# 56

I knew

We'd always be a blasphemy

We always mixed emotions,

With our drinks,

From the very start.

Now we're drunk

With each other's words,

Lost somewhere between

Too far to reach out to.

Too near,

To not give it another shot.

# 57

Let me take a mud bath today,
A sea salt bath,
I light my candles
My incense
And soak rose petals in the tub,
I play soft music,
And slowly
Let my hair come down,
Touching my shoulders,
Touching my skin.
The water is just warm enough
To slightly burn my skin
Turning it into patches of red,
Here and there.
I scan my body and notice
I've been bitten by some insect
On either side of my waist,
And my left thigh.
I raise my feet,
To take a plunge
But it looks like the water's already cold.
Because the whole time
I was typing poetry,

With some bubbles on my hands.

# 58

Am I this loneliness

Or is this loneliness me,

Because I am sure we aren't two different entities.

# 59

He left you in the storm,
What makes you think
He is the source of your sun.

# 60

Two star-crossed lovers,
One shines by the day,
And the other by the night.
Cosmic beings
Scattered all over the sky.
Sometimes the comet you wish upon,
Other times the storm you curse upon.
We may be a galaxy of ironies,
But my soul has known yours
Ever since the very beginning of time.
For we're made from the same stars
And we carry the same celestial scars.
And when we were born on earth
It was nothing less than a miracle,
How would you otherwise put it?
A cosmic reunion
A love,
That just stood the test of time
Or a serendipity?

# 61

Not every person who says they love you means it,
Not everyone who bids you goodbye wants to leave.

# 62

The reason why I feel so empty is because,
When you chased me away
From the home I had built in you,
These feet took the body away,
But the heart was stubborn enough to stay.

# 63

Take me far,
This city is tainted with your love,
The trees that had our names inscribed,
Is fading, time has it healing.
The wind still blows in glee,
Not knowing we are in love any more.
It has stopped raining,
It's November already,
Winter already, Wednesday already.
Let's hide our face,
Because every nook
From the brightly lit up markets
To the deserted streets,
They only scream your name.
The birds in chorus,
Rehearse the lament song.
The roses are dried,
The thorns are sharpened
To redraw the scars,
The map of the city,
We fell in love with,
We fell in love.
There are a hundred million things I would say,

Sorry, goodbye…..
Like scattered stars in the sky.
I keep forgetting the names of constellations,
But you're scorpion,
Hundred things I wanna say,
But let's not scream, let's not fight anymore,
No worries, no goodbyes ….
Let the birds warble,
Let the city talk,
For it knows more,
Don't let this city know,
We're in love no more.
Let's just pretend.

# 64

Only a heart
That is made of stone
Will break
Into a thousand pieces
For you.
A heart that is soft
Will at the most
Only cry.

# 65

Dancing in a field of rain lilies
Daisies in your hair
And sunflowers in your
Torn jean pocket
The sky is a lavender blue,
And Iris the colour of your eyes.
Life seems so much better
When viewed through
A rose-tinted glass.
Azalea marked the start of winter
And in the foggy haze of December
My words hang like ivy
From my violet lips,
My heart is a garden
Of a thousand chrysanthemums
And amid it lay an unfathomable grief.

# 66

My body is a holiday destination.
So come have a good time in,
Nobody goes for vacations forever,
So when you are rejuvenated enough,
And ready to leave,
Take a hair,
Take a nail,
Or an eyelash,
As your holiday souvenir.
So that every time you see it,
You are remembered
Of our gala times,
Yearning for that kiss,
In that little country town,
But it's only in your remembrance,
I am an exotic destination,
For I too am old,
A tattered city now.
Tired of entertaining,
Never ending lads like you.
Looking for a day off like you.

# 67

Perhaps,
Love wasn't enough
I had to give you
Dead flowers
And poetry.

# 68

Hearts,
As if commodities
Wanting to be brought and sold.

# 69

I would rather,
Be the moon
Than your sun
For you never
Look into the eye of the sun.

# 70

It takes a lot to be somebody's sunshine.
When you give light,
You will know what surviving in the shadow feels like.
I let you become the light,
That blinds me.
While I sit in the darkness.
Providing you with warmth.
By burning chunks of me.
It feels like I've lost my eyesight,
The bones have become cold,
The feet are numb.
But with this smile on my face.
I linger on.
You seem distant and full of vigour
You shine,
Your brightness even blinding yourself,
Making me invisible to you.
You want more,
And I scrape the corners of my windows,
The tiny holes on my tin roof.
And all the little places,
Where specks of light entered my soul.
I empty them all to give it to you.

Yet you come back,
Always hungry again,
Dull again, dimmed again.
I want more again.
You say my eyes aren't desirable anymore.
It's shallow when you look into them,
But darling when all you're engulfed by
Is darkness,
Isn't a well-meant to look shallow?

# 71

Sometimes
What you ask for
Is so less,
They will never
Give it to you.

# 72

Sometimes
You just want to
Wear your old clothes.
And go back
To the same old people
Even if you look ugly
Even if they break your heart.

# 73

With this hollow in my heart,
I feel empty now.
As if engulfed by the black hole,
That's nowhere but in me.
When I walk the alleys,
The silence is terrifying
I can hear my own heart beating,
My gasps echoing.
You cry my name.
You are calling for me,
But the closer I go towards you,
The further I go into the dark,
The black hole pulling me.
Pushing you farther off.
Its dark but I am not scared anymore,
It's white and cold,
Lifeless and colourless here,
The silence that once terrified
Now brings in comfort.
I have lost sense of time,
I don't know how long I've remained.
Seems like yesterday,
Seems like forever.

I still scream your name,

Hoping you'll hear me.

But no voice comes,

I've lost speech,

Though the memory still is crisp and clear.

I can't craft your face.

I remember you left, you're gone,

Leaving me with this hollow in my heart.

And in that hole

I'm still collecting myself

Like the shards of a broken glass.

# 74

My heart is broken,
So be gentle with it
Not because it will break further,
But because the harsher you get
The deeper you will cut yourself.

# 75

All the while,
You thought it was okay
for you to be treated like thrash,
But it's a dangerous thing,
To be in the wrong hands,
A gem can easily
Be undervalued.

# 76

I am in my half phase
But I'll soon be whole
The light me me vary
But that's just me
As seen from your side
Of the world,
I go through light and dark stages,
But I know I'm always whole.

# 77

Maybe she is not whole,
Maybe she is all fragments,
Of her broken past,
Holding each piece
With a brave heart.

THE RETURNING

# 78

Sometimes you need to,
Get away from home,
Sometimes to get back.

# 79

When the sun shone,
The light hit you first,
In places where you held your
darkest secrets,
The places you were too afraid of,
To show the world.
Open your eyes,
See the dark spaces,
Flowers are blooming in there,
The only thing,
Keeping you alive.
Now don't be stupid,
Don't ask how the flowers bloomed
Without light air and water
You never knew,
But you had it all in you,
The air, the water, the love and the light.

# 80

How can I take it slow?
I have missed you everyday,
For three years now,
I could drink you in a gulp.
Kiss you through the night
Embrace you in my arms,
So tiny, disappearing like a snowball,
By the warmth of my skin.
And we finally,
In the act of becoming one.

# 81

You're lost and stranded
Searching for a place
That actually
And only resides in you .

# 82

Letting go isn't easy,
But sometimes you have to,
Not for anyone,
This time it's to save your soul.

# 83

For how long do you want me to mourn?
The anger has dissipated,
The storm has settled,
The grief is gone,
A long time
Not long enough for you.
But after all these years of pain
I finally see the face of healing,
The warmth of self love,
The power of patience
And it's strange
But the thing that wrecks your heart
And the thing that brings you
Hope and light
Is but the same force.

# 84

When you mishandle her
And take her for her soft petals
She will pierce your back with her nails
She is forced to grow
To tame those filthy hands
But she wasn't always like that
A rose is never born with thorns.

# 85

He wakes up at night,
To give you your notebook and pen,
To write that poem,
You would otherwise
Never write in sleep.
He gives you love bites,
Your high necks are too low to cover,
He gives you a love,
You don't want to hide.
And when he comes near,
Your eyes close,
Yearning for that kiss,
The warmth of his breath,
His whispers on your ears,
His hands on your hips.

# 86

Take it slow,
I am not in a rush,
I stop by every cherry tree,
Just to admire its beauty.
And when I'm gone past it,
I still have the time to,
Turn back at it,
And write a full length poem on it,
So take it slow,
For it takes a whole fall of autumn,
The naked shame of winter,
And a whole cycle of seasons,
Before it's spring once again
And the cherries can bloom again.

# 87

It took you so long to realise
You're the home
You've been searching for
All the while.
But it's okay
The doors will always open
For you,
Because you hold the key.

# 88

You're a bundle of energy
But your calmness
Is that like the sea.
You're the sailor,
You're the master,
You're a creator,
Of the universe.
You are it's beings,
You are strong,
Yet soft
You are powerful,
Yet easy to defeat.
You are enormous,
But just an atom you are
Born from the center of the earth
From dust,
And in dust
You shall again perish.

# 89

When it twinkles,
That's when I believe in magic,
Sometimes it's the stars,
Other times it's your eyes.

# 90

I am but a half-read book
Forgotten on a corner shelf
Collecting dust
Day by day.
Yet I stay,
With a hope that someday you'll return
When you've run out of hardbacks and first editions,
And maybe I'm not a classic,
But perhaps,
In those folded corners
Of my pages,
There is a part of me
You did love,
And will someday would want to return to.

# 91

But how could I ever be yours,
And how could you ever be mine?
There is only one place
We belong
And that is to ourselves.

# 92

My eyes are fierce
But I am softer than I seem,
I too have suffered.
Even though I didn't scream.

# 93

How can I put you in words,
This is just a vain attempt,
I could drown in your eyes
Its vastness is that of the universe,
And also the unknown beyond.

# 94

Like a cup of coffee on a rainy day,
A cozy blanket on a snowy afternoon,
Your fluffy cardigan that smells of sleep
I wish to envelope you in a tight embrace
That is what
I call home.

# 95

When it twinkles,
That's when I believe in magic,
Sometimes it's the stars,
Other times it's your eyes.

# 96

It isn't easy to forgive,
The ones who have wronged us,
But it isn't as hard as carrying,
That hate in your heart.
For the rest of your life.

# 97

As long as there is music

Flowing in this room,

Motion in our bones

And mourning in our soul.

We are here.

As long as the music lasts,

But let's dance slow,

To the rhythm,

Like forever is ours,

Let's know each other so deep.

It will take a lifetime to forget.

Even though we will be

No more familiar,

No less stranger,

Walking out of here,

Than walking in here.

This is a small world,

Different from the world outside,

To where we belong.

But for now this is where we belong

Me in your arms,

Your face in my eyes,

And the music slowly fading from our ears.

# 98

The world never runs out of good people
But it is true
That sometimes,
People are bad
Because they forget
That they are at heart
Good.

# 99

I wrote you a song
But since
I can't sing
I called it a poem.

# 100

I am a wrecked ship
That's sinking in the ocean,
Come save me,
But I'll drown anyway,
Come drown with me,
Let's go away from this cruel world,
That's only taught us to hate.
Let's sink.
I believe
There's heaven down there.
In the underworld.
Where we can all
Learn to love.

# 101

When I say that I am a poet
It is only a part of what I actually am
What I don't say is
I am hurting,
I am healing,
I am not just making
But becoming a work of art.

# 102

If we were all seasons,
Tell me what would I be?
You'd be winter obviously,
Not meaning you're cold,
Your hands produced sweat,
So it could warm mine.
But it's true you never let
Your guard down,
Those fences protecting your heart,
The stiffness of your body,
The softening of your heart
Like melting of ice,
It's the winter sun,
Bringing a slight warmth
In the glistening of your eyes,
Like the breaking of ice.
White face,
Reddened cheeks,
Tell me what else would you be?
If not the season of snow?

# 103

Our bones will not tire,
Our Hearts shall not fail
Seeking for companionship.
But perhaps we are all lonely,
Looking for another lonely being,
To fill our soul with,
To be friends with.
To hear and share stories with.

# 104

In the directness of the scorching sun
The worker with his sickle,
Pulls out the creeping weeds,
From the wall of the rich man.
A man on a bench
Under the shade of trees
Watches him,
Gossiping with his friend.
A pedestrian walking,
Sometimes in the direct sun,
Sometimes under the shade of trees
The man and men.
But they soon are out of her sight,
The picture still crisp in her head,
The thoughts still lingering.
She realises it's only from a distance,
The bigger picture is seen with clarity.

# 105

We will love with all our hearts
Because we've been deprived of it
Ourselves.

# 106

Even when it rains,
And the mornings
Become slightly cold,
There is something
About Autumn
That warms the soul
And feels like home.

# 107

City lights gleamed
As if mirroring the galaxy above
She looked up at the sky
A canvas of blankness
A blanket of blackness
To lose herself into
But she didn't want to get lost
She wanted to find herself
Amongst the stars
But there were none
Not one she could spot
Not two she could talk to
He looked down at the city lights
A work of art they were
Neon flickers
To cozy candlelight diners
She gazed at it till her vision blurred
Strange but the light that makes you see
Blinds you too
Like a counterfeit currency
Shiny and new
But darling
It was dirt clothed in purity.

# 108

When I've risen enough
Let me also know,
How to descend like a yellow leaf.
Falling without hesitation
Without the slightest regret.
Returning back to earth
From where it was birthed.
The whole process
Is not even called
Detaching
But simply
A Homecoming.

# 109

Darling why do you want to fit in
And feel left out
The universe is vast,
Run around it
Like it is your own garden
And spring has come.

# 110

Your cheeks are like roses
Water painted with rain drops
Your perfume intoxicates you
And you're still running.
But who is it you're away from
Is it them,
Or is it yourself from the past ?
They've already forgotten your middle name
And won't recognise you,
In a sea of strangers.
When all they are doing
Is sitting on a bench opposite
Looking at people.
You've forgotten you're wearing any perfume
Until the wind blows along.
Nobody knows
But only the cigarette butt can tell
That our lips had once touched.
In the golden hour,
Nobody notices but even flowers petals
Are uneven in shape and colour.
The birds rest too,
And grief bothers me too.

You don't have enough cash to run away from home
So just book a cab
And return,
Where your heart does not belong
In the evenings it is still cold,
In the mornings you need an extra blanket.
Who are you waiting for?
Is it him?
Or your future self to take you away from your past.

# 111

Maybe I will never
Meet your expectations of me,
And I'll never be,
Who you want me to be,
But it's okay,
I'm a moon-child,
And oh! she loves me for it.

# 112

She loved the rain
And the thunderstorms
Because that's all she was familiar with
In her heart.

# 113

Tangerine eyes,

Oh! Did you eat the sun?

How mirror sharp,

It reflects

All of my heart's ugly corners

You bring light

But when you're you've been gone for years now,

And all I'm used to is darkness

Oh! Tangerine eyes,

Tell me, tell me,

Isn't it the sun that's the source of darkness,

Isn't darkness now my light?

# 114

Maybe we just
Have our darkest days,
So that we learn
To appreciate the light,
Even the tiniest source,
Even the moon,
Even the stars.

# 115

Sometimes,
I don't believe in love,
But in your eyes
When you talk about,
The things you love,
I think I saw it there,
Something very close to love.

# 116

And when you are ready to drown
Even the sea will be
Gentle with you.
For now you have trusted its waters
To take you offshore.

# 117

Only the pedestrians
Know of shortcuts,
Through the middle of the wood,
Littered with red seasonal blossoms
And the entering of light,
Through leaves, the shape of needles,
The hustle in the silence,
Of a falling autumn leaf.
And her footsteps,
Softer than the last time,
Due to the wearing of her shoes.
And the distant noises,
Of which she is aware of,
But pays no heed to,
For all she needs,
Is a little time alone,
In nature,
To heal, to feel,
One with the creator's
Marvellous creations.

# 118

Autumn
Makes every leaf on every tree fall,
And yet it's strange
How it is the only season
I am most grateful for.

# 119

Let the fire in you light, warm,
But let it also not be afraid to rage, to burn everything
down.

# 120

Why has the rain ceased
And the flowers returned
Why does the chirping bird
Sound so happy
At the sight of the fooling sun?
I crave for the October winds,
And the crispy September leaves.
I crave for carefree days,
And nights catching stars.
Oh, ugly Summer!
Wake me up when you're gone.
No, I don't want to look pretty
With white daisies in my head
And dresses that just hit the thighs.
Promise me a slower August,
And the longest November nights.

# THE HEALING

# 121

Let us learn,
To not hold back,
The things that aren't meant for us,
Let us gently let them go,
So that there is new room,
For you to grow.

# 122

She not just writes poetry,
She is poetry,
Every bit of her is art
Like the sun, the stars and her scars.

# 123

When autumn comes,
And leaves fall,
It brings about,
In people,
This hope for spring.

# 124

Slow down,
Let's not run,
The race beyond the finish line.
Let's not forget,
You can't be everything,
Before it's your time.

# 125

You're not a difficult person,
You just need a little more time,
A little more space,
A little more love,
That has been robbed from you
And hands that will be gentle with you.

# 126

You radiate light
Even after being
In the darkness for so long.
Because the light was not around you,
The light was always there,
Inside of you.

# 127

Out of the midnight stars,
You were born.
The sun bows down,
The day dawns,
And darkness takes over,
To remind you,
Of that light you embody.

# 128

Our hearts are too heavy
Carrying the names of those who left us
Years ago.
When a lover leaves,
Your heart deserves peace.
So when it's time for them to go
Write their names
On flower petals instead
Blow them away like birds
Set them free
And only then
You'll be.

# 129

Remember you will fall out of love
With so many people
Only to fall deeper in love with yourself.

# 130

In all its shapes half a full
The moon is loved and so are you.

# 131

No matter how much
People have wronged us
Departures need not be devastations,
You are not them,
And you will for the last time,
Teach them how kindness works,
By just bidding a sweet goodbye.

# 132

You need not look at
The sun in the eye,
To know it's there,
The light, the warmth,
Teaches you,
To trust
Even on the rainiest days.

# 133

Sometimes
You fall apart
So that you can put the pieces together
Your way.

# 134

I was so reluctant to let some things go
That I held onto it tight
Till my joints numbed
And my fingers got blisters
Exposing my heart,
Just red and ugly
The colour of my soul
When I lost you
For you used to roam so freely in my mind
Rendering me homeless.
You made all my writings about you
Like you were me,
And I was you.
And when you were gone
I thought I'd lose a part of me too
This fear of becoming someone
I no longer knew,
But now I am me
Only true
And I would not have been
Who I am today
Had I not untangled the knots
That bound us,

And let you become you.

# 135

My mystery baffles you,
My calmness scares you,
My love makes you wanting for more.
I was born that way,
And the moon is my mother.

# 136

Healing was about,
Picking your pieces up
Even if you're not able to
Put them back together.

# 137

Your light may get dimmed at times
But I promise,
You'll never
Lose your path.

# 138

Whether we like it or not,
Sometimes the weight of memories
Becomes so heavy
We need to put it down
Like a burden.

# 139

I learnt something very late in my life
And that something is self-love.
How could I have given love to the people around me,
All my life,
I had deprived myself of it.
And all those empty feelings I had
Were maybe meant to be there
Only to teach me
To fill my heart with this brimming love,
Maybe I was always meant to be that way- Empty,
But then I never understood,
That the usefulness of a cup lay in that very emptiness.
You are enough
And it's now time to fill your cup.
With the right water,
That replenishes your soul,
Overcomes your fears,
Heals your wounds,
And washes away your tears.

# 140

No matter how much you love someone,
You can never make them yours,
Because they are always their's,
And they can never make you theirs,
For you are always yours,
Just like I am always mine.

# 141

How can you be a bad person
Just because
Someone can't see
The goodness in you.

# 142

Sometimes,
What you go through,
Is so dirty,
That art is born out of it.

Like
A lotus,
Symbolising purity,
Is born out of the muddy waters.

# 143

It will never be quite alright,
But it will never be so bad,
That you can't make it through.

# 144

I know it's heavy
But you have to let it go
Like it is a balloon.

# 145

You left a hole,
Where there was once a crack,
The size of your heart,
But don't worry about me,
It no longer make me cold at night,
That's where the sun hits me first
Every morning.

# 146

Be patient.
The earth is round,
Healing will find you like war did.

# 147

There's a demon
Living in my heart,
Running in my mind
Even when it's late
I tell her go to sleep
But she needs no rest
She shows me my insecurities
And the wrinkles on my face,
But today,
I do not feed her,
Nor eat what she cooks,
Nor listen to what she has to say.

# 148

Don't be arrogant
You've only seen
The parts of me
I've revealed to you
The moon is not always calming
But how will you know?
You've not for once seen her
Cause the tides.

# 149

You will never be able to hurt me again
Not because
I've mastered the art of healing.
But simply because
I have learnt
To love myself.

# 150

Even if the past has been
Extremely bitter
And you miss the ones
Who have
Brought you pain
It's true
You will always meet people
Who you will come to
Love and trust
Because it's not just deceit
The world is filled with
It's kindness too.

# 151

Where there is a will,
There is a way,
Where there is hurting,
Healing is on the way.

# 152

You were broken,
Not to be fixed by others,
But to heal on your own.

# 153

How can you ever be
Enough for the ones,
Who only looked at you
Like you were half?

# 154

Let the fire in you light, warm,
But let it also not be afraid to rage, to burn everything
down.

# 155

You know why the heart is a beautiful thing
It is only because
It tends to break
And yet,
Be whole again.

# 156

Because superheroes aren't real,
Only poets will save the world.

# 157

Grief struck you
But how was waiting
For you
Like a bud
To open up.

# 158

How can you please everyone
Even the sun
At one point of time
Can only
Light up one half of the earth.

# 159

There are days
You haven't lived,
And nights you haven't wept,
There are hearts
You haven't loved,
And love you haven't felt,
Some forevers do last
And promises
That won't fail
And it is there
You belong.

# 160

A writers heart is a beautiful thing
But it cannot be tamed.
When she cries
It rains.
And when she hurts
Poems sprout
Everywhere like mushrooms.

# 161

Will giving new names
To old wounds make it any better?
If tomorrow I suddenly said,
"My grief is not grief,
It's a gun
My words the bullets
My poems
A battle of words."

# 162

My story need not
Resonate with yours
We've both been broken
And I will hold you
Like your mother does.

# 163

I would rather
Be the dirt
Under your feet
Firming your roots,
And the water,
Seeping through
The rocks
To nourish your soul,
Than being
The wind
Which makes your flowers flutter,
And the sun,
Towards whom
You turn to.
I would rather
Love you passionately in silence,
Than to love you loud,
In front of the whole world.

# 164

Healing always comes
With arms wide open
But it's useless,
Until you too
Stretch out
From the other end.

# 165

When time comes
The bud will burst open
Into a flower
That brings joy
The sun and the rain that poured on you
Wasn't to kill you
But you make you bloom.

# 166

What's firmness,
What's frailty?
The storm that can
Uproot a tree
And demolish a house,
But can't crush a wildflower
It's tender, frail petals.

# 167

Lazy mornings,
Mellow days,
You're the home
I return to.
A full garden
Wickedly blooming,
The smell of coffee
I don't drink,
And unmade beds.
You're a moody lover
But in the presence of cold
Your warmth still is better.
This summer romance
Has come to an end
The sun has set
And your dancing silhouette
Has found her home
In an ocean full of stars
To drown into
And maybe, just maybe
To get some rest.

# 168

October taught me:-

To Fall is beautiful, there is no shame in nakedness but bravery.

# 169

Even in my rotting body,
Flowers bloomed,
And that's when I realised,
How much I'm loved.

# 170

When the heart breaks
Some pieces shatter so far
That they no longer
Belong to you,
They are outside of your body
And won't take you for it's home
You got to let them go
And build with the remains
And it will take you by surprise
That you can still be whole
The power darling
Was in letting go.

# 171

Healing myself,

Was never about hating you,

Or forgetting you,

It was just the opposite,

Healing was being able to still remember you,

And love you,

But without feeling any pain,

You brought it along.

# 172

I have been broken so often,
That falling in love scares me
I no longer
Write my poems
With a pen
But a knife with a sharp edge.

Oh! Luna
You hear my heart,
It's only you,
Who read my poems
And understands how I feel tonight.

I am pouring my heart out
On your white sheets
On this cold wintry night.

The moon is red,
From the poems stained with blood,
So are the sheets,
But it's only once a month,
The tides are caused.

Today I don't care for summers
Nor the long daylight.
But tomorrow the moon will be white again
A blank canvas to draw on
And maybe I would have healed
As well as learnt how to hold a pen once again.

# 173

Some people leave and your heart breaks,
But know that is the exact moment your heart is saved.

# 174

Some days
You just don't have the strength
To fight.
On such days,
Know that you're a warrior
To just survive.

# 175

To the child
That is healing inside me
I will listen to the story
Every cell of yours
Is bursting to say,
I will let you cry
And wipe your tears
Off with my hair
I will hold you in my lap
And fold you in my arms
Till the wounds have sealed
And your heart has healed.

# 176

And just like that
One fine morning,
The heart just felt easy to walk away.
Light as match stick boxes.
Nothing holding it back,
Nothing holding it down.

# 177

Even on days
You're not full
Remember you're the moon
And you'll always be beautiful.

# 178

Don't close the door,
For the ones who wish to leave.
Hold it open,
And watch them leave.
Nothing could have made them stay,
They would have broken the door anyway.

# 179

You thought it was
The end of the world
But how the sun
Kept rising
Day after day
To make you believe
You too were meant to rise.

# 180

Today,
I thanked the wildflowers
That bloomed
Even after being stomped upon.
And scattered by the wind
I asked them
How they did that
And they replied
That's how they are made
Not for pots and vases
But for the cracks in between the walls
And all the other broken places.

# About The Author

*Meet Denmit Lepcha, or Den as she prefers to be called. She's not just an avid reader, but also a promising poet in the world of writing in the hills. Her book, Lee, is a collection of poems that beautifully captures the journey towards self-discovery and finding one's true home. Despite not being a fan of series and movies, one thing she absolutely adores is gardening in her abode nestled in the picturesque mountains of Dzongu, North Sikkim.*

www.ingramcontent.com/pod-product-compliance
Lightning Source LLC
Chambersburg PA
CBHW021352150726
47989CB00005B/2219